I0410408

Frog Coloring Book For Adults

30 Hand Drawn, Doodle and Folk Art Style Frog Adult Coloring Pages

By
Louise Ford

ISBN-13: 978-1539854388
ISBN-10: 1539854388

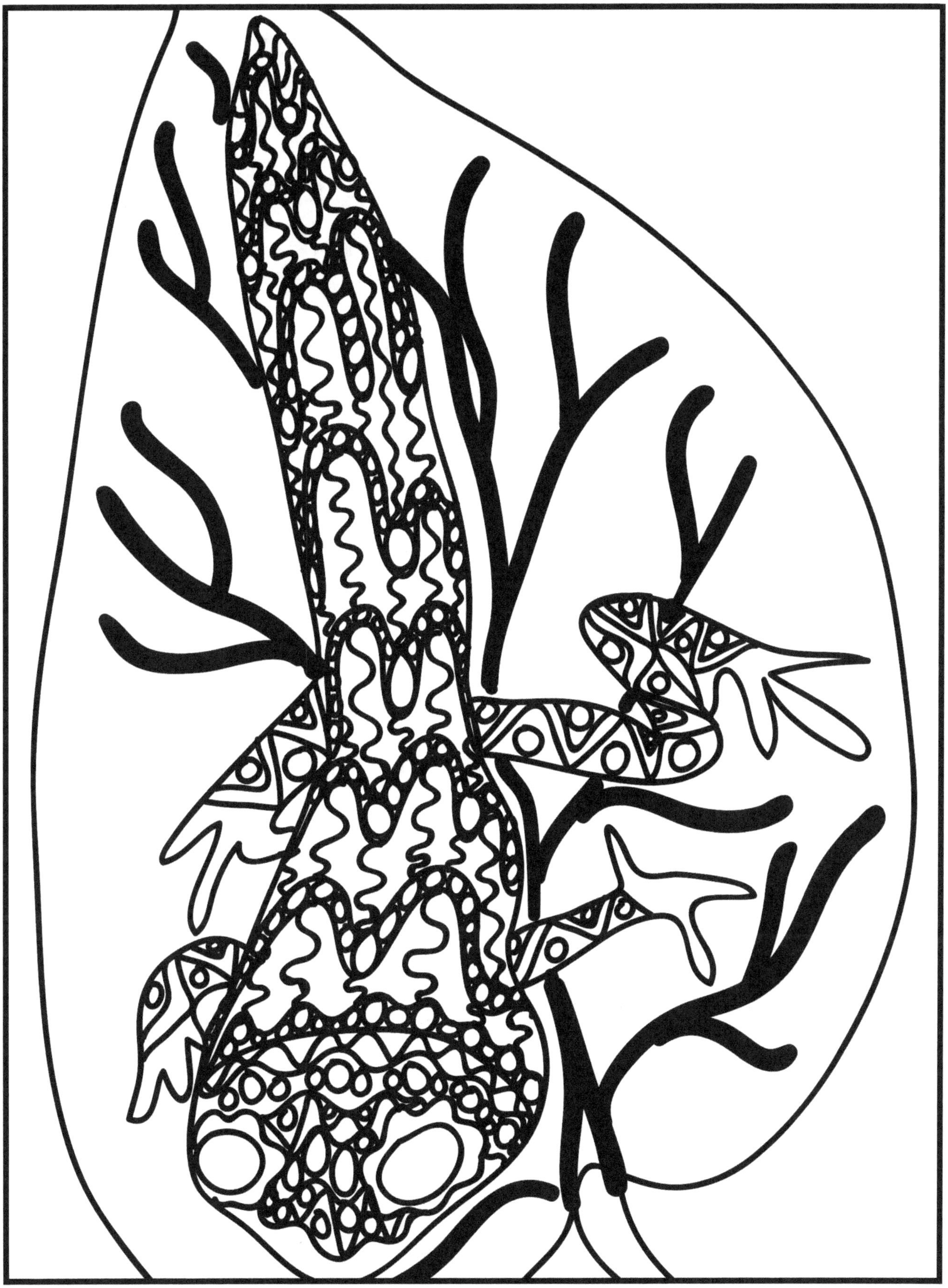

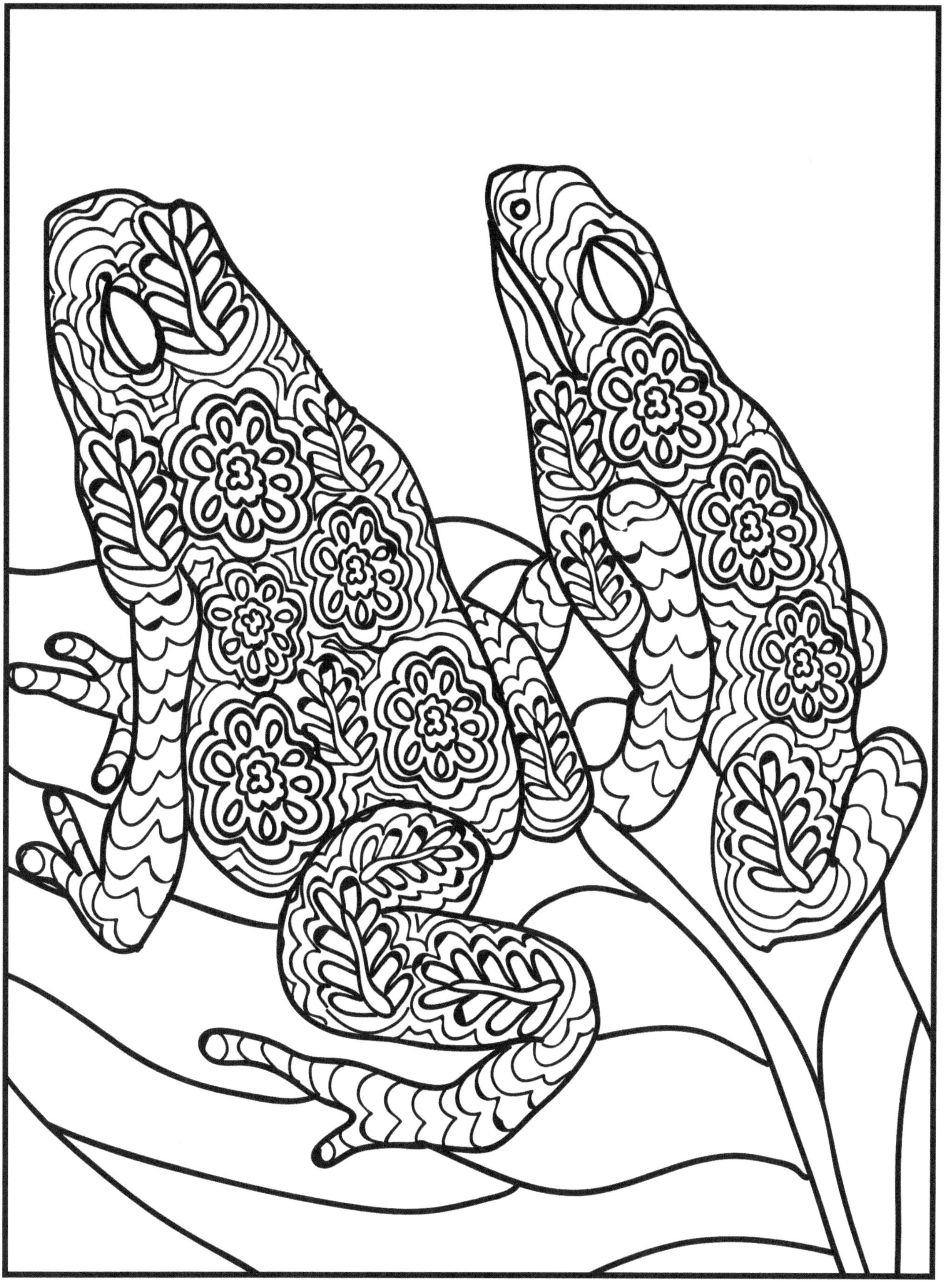

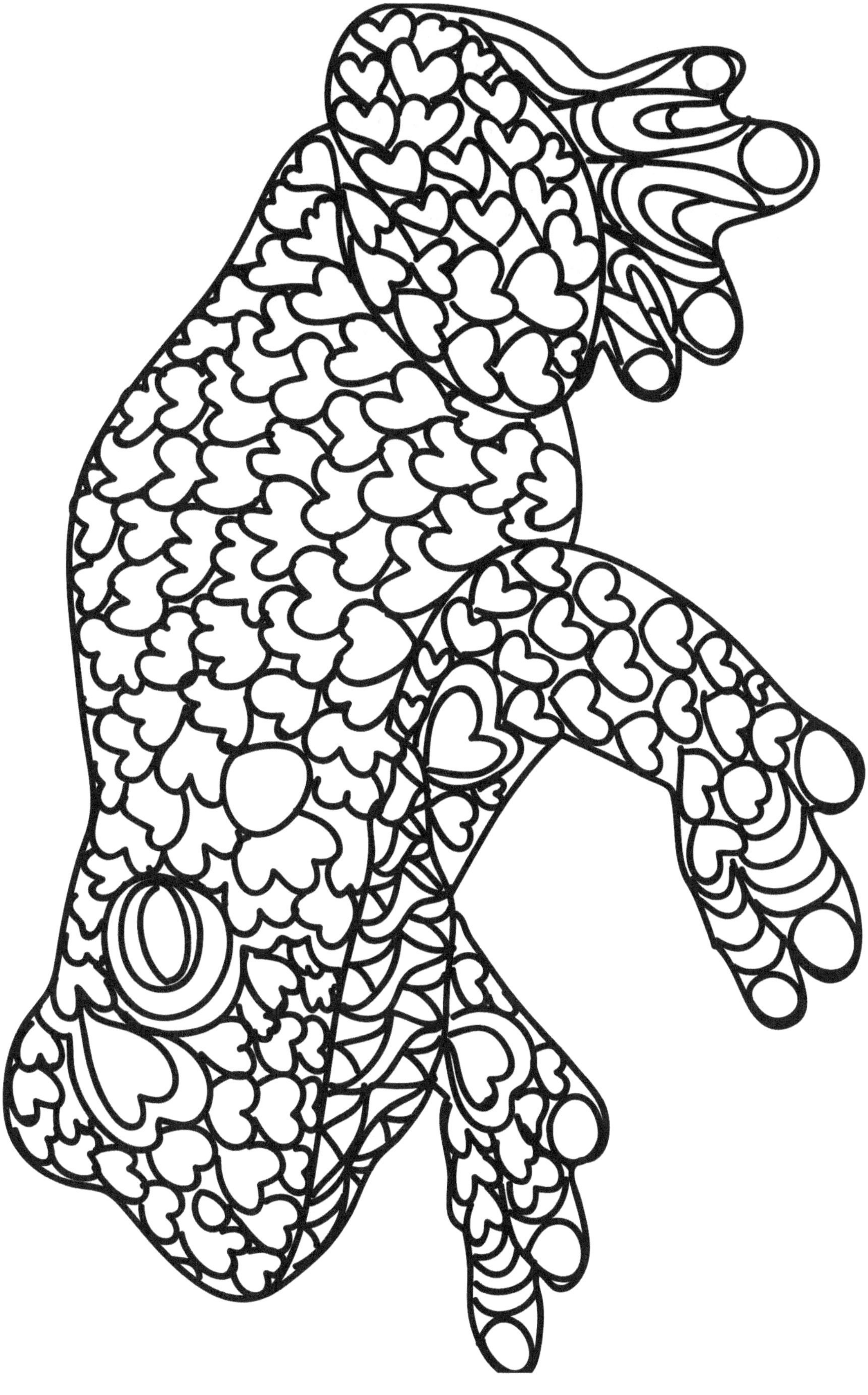

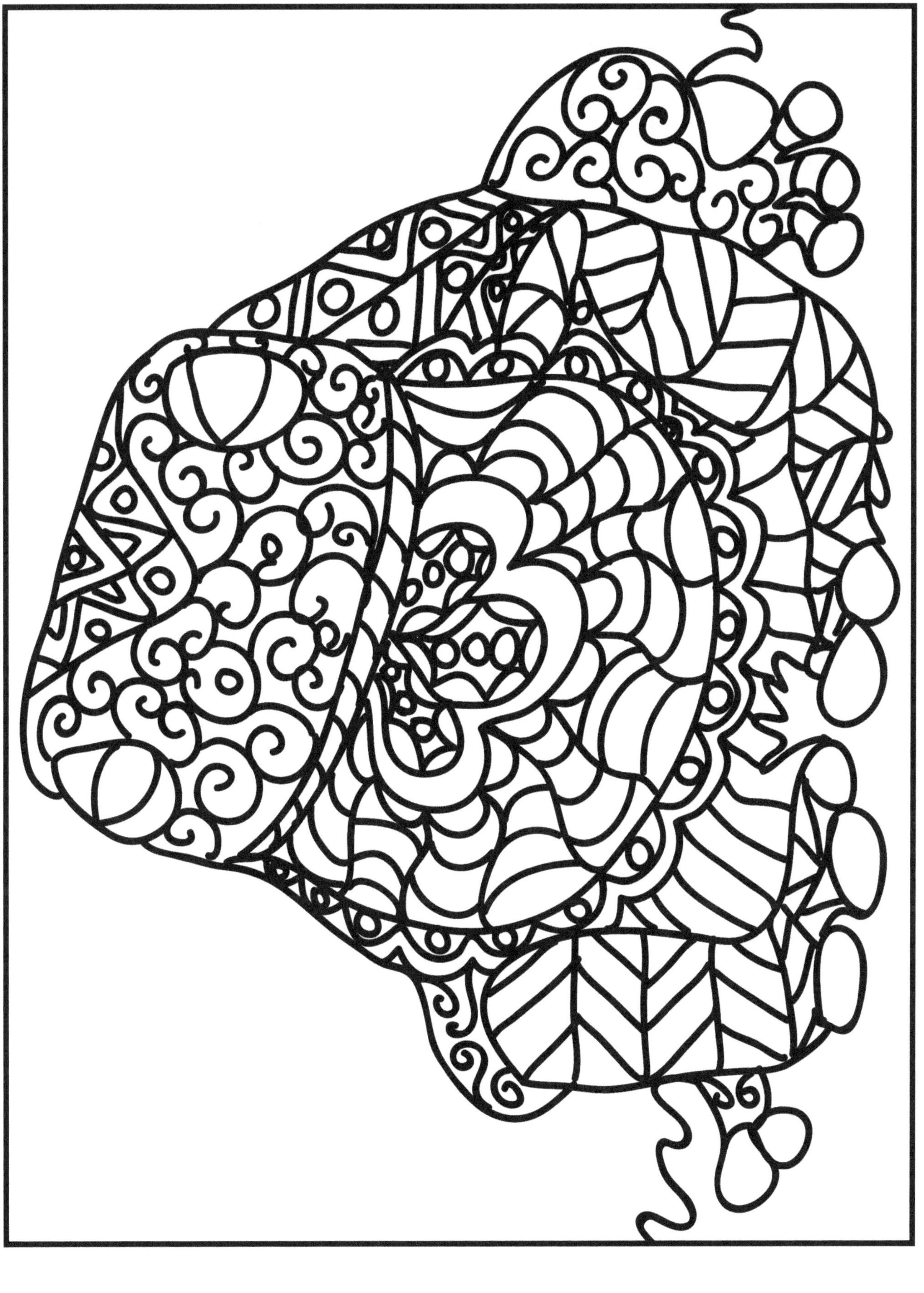
3

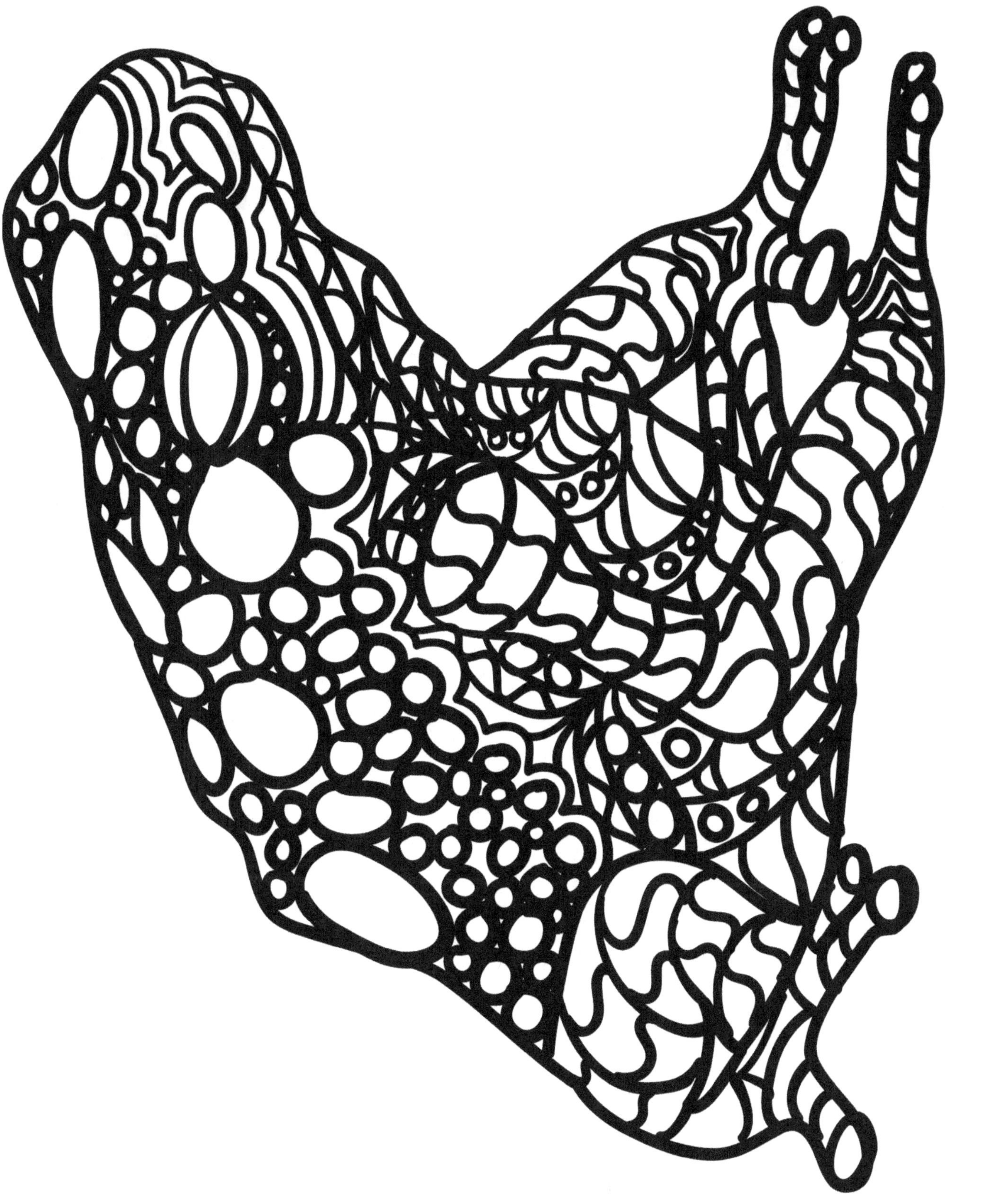

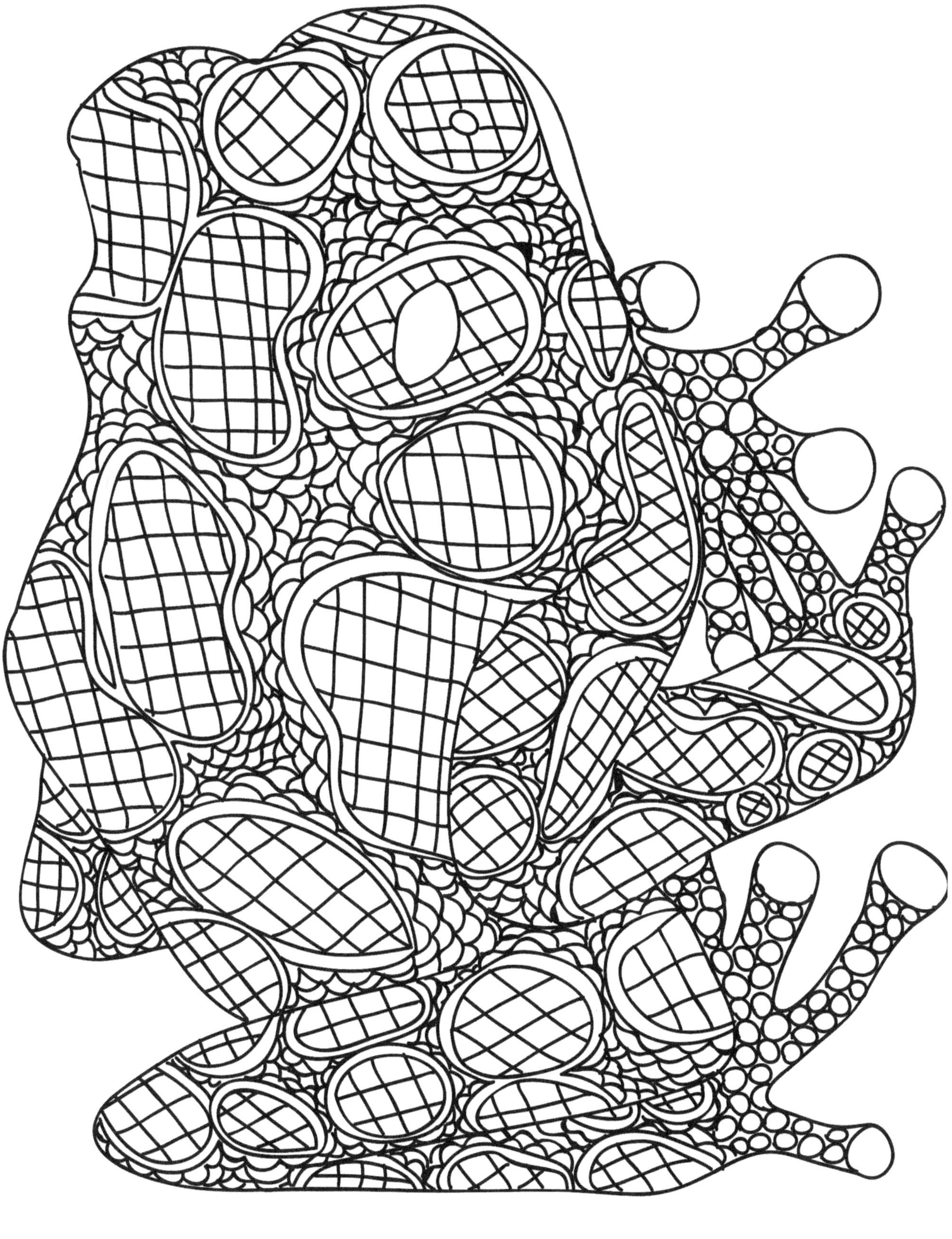

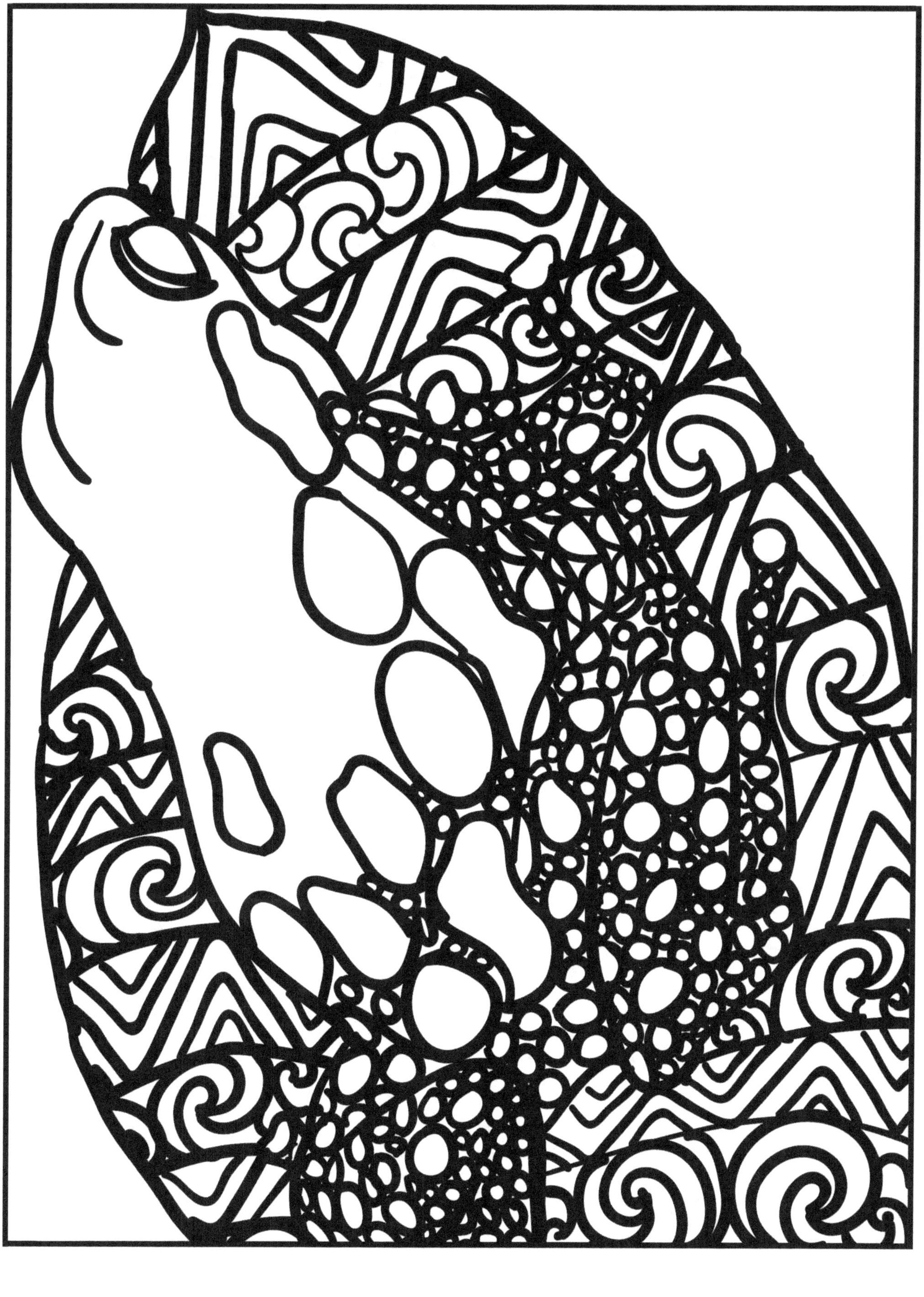

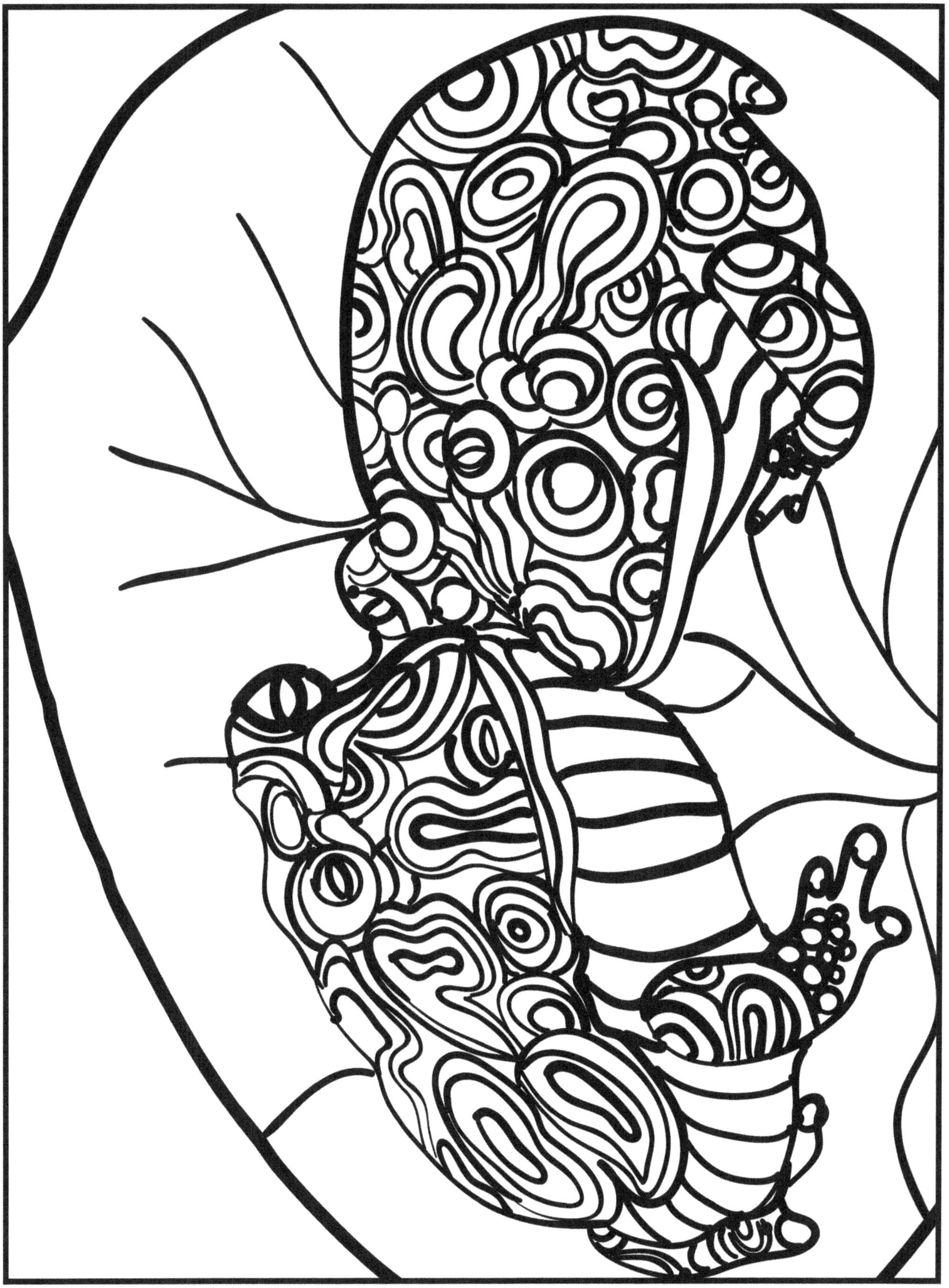

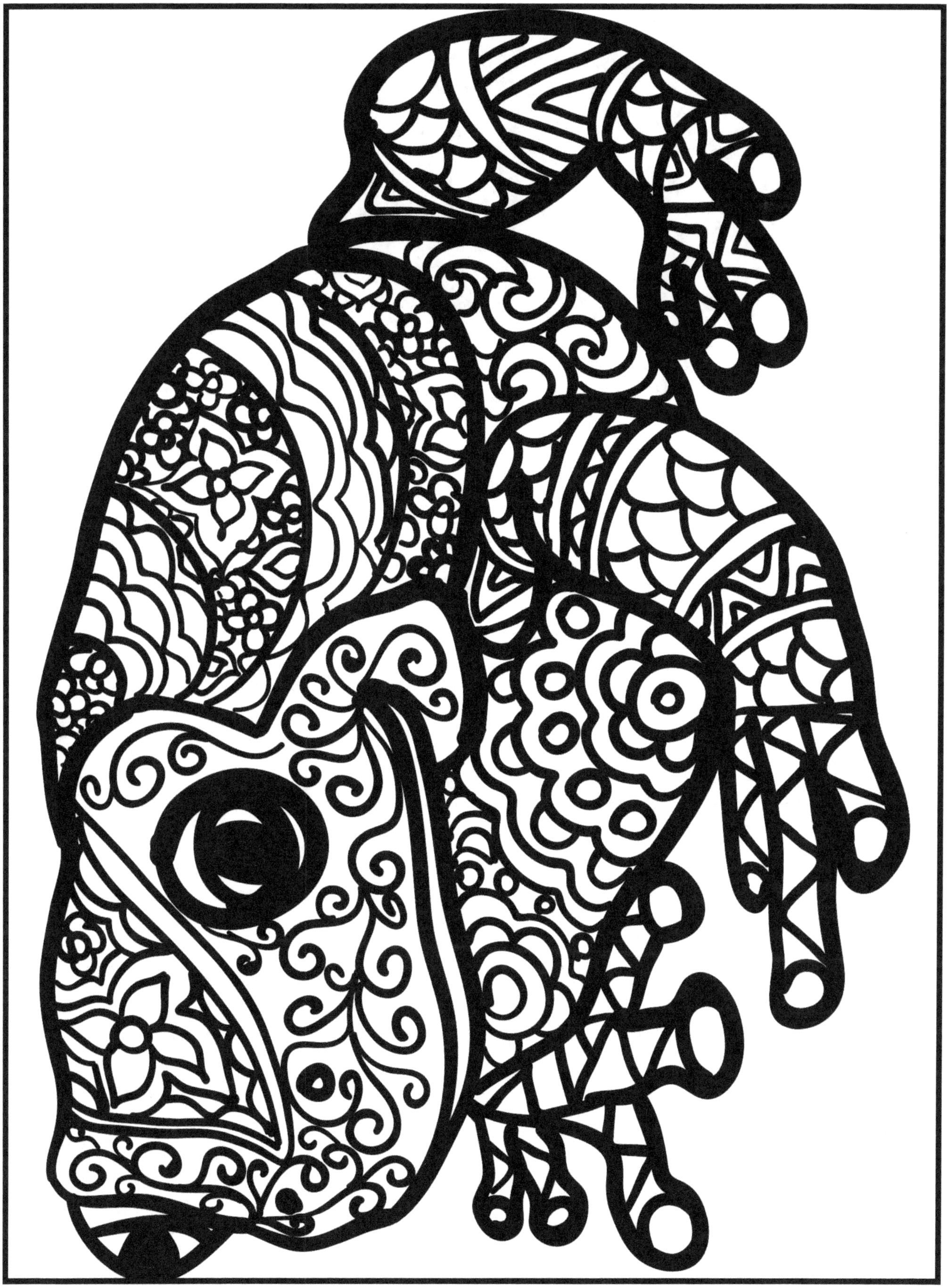

www.ingramcontent.com/pod-product-compliance
Lightning Source LLC
Chambersburg PA
CBHW081859280526
45789CB00007B/2761
9781539854388